DEAN ATTA

I Am Nobody's Nigger

The Westbourne Press

Published 2013 by The Westbourne Press

1

© Dean Atta 2013

ISBN 978-1-908906-16-8
eISBN 978-1-908906-17-5

Printed and bound by CPI Group (UK) Ltd, Croydon, CRO 4YY

The Westbourne Press
26 Westbourne Grove, London W2 5RH
www.westbournepress.co.uk

Dean Atta is a writer and performance poet. He has been commissioned to write poems for the Damilola Taylor Trust, Keats House Museum, National Portrait Gallery, Tate Britain and Tate Modern. Atta won the 2012 London Poetry Award and was named as one of the most influential LGBT people by the Independent on Sunday Pink List 2012. An ambassador for the Spirit of London Awards, he lives in London and teaches writing workshops across the UK.

www.deanatta.co.uk
@DeanAtta

'When young writers ask me for tips I tell them that the greatest ingredient you should have in your poetry is honesty, and Dean Atta's poetry is as honest as truth itself. He follows no trend, he seeks no favours, this is him. He is his biggest influence. Beyond black, beyond white, beyond straight, beyond gay, so I say. Love your eyes over these words of truth. You will be uplifted.' Benjamin Zephaniah

'With this superb collection, Dean has inherited the spiritual key of black penned poetry from its previous keeper, Benjamin Zephaniah, and successfully used it to unlock the door of truths.' Norman Jay MBE

'Righteous and forceful' Peter Tatchell

'Dean Atta is a man on a mission ... one of the most outspoken social commentators of his musical generation' Tom Robinson, BBC 6 Music

'Poetry is a powerful tool, and *I Am Nobody's Nigger* is a perfect example of when that tool shows its full strength.' *Huffington Post*

'Raconteur Dean Atta doing what he does best; articulating London's dark, deep-rooted social cancers through a beautiful and intricately personal narrative' *Clash*

'A spoken word master' *Hackney Hive*

'One of the UK's finest poets' *Time Out*

Contents

Forty Things I Never Said

Well done
I believe in you
I'm proud of you
You don't know me as well as you think you do
Every missed opportunity burns me
I never loved you
You are wrong
I haven't forgiven you
It was only sex
No strings attached
I think you should go now
When I left you that night, I cried
I care more about the things I have lost
When I told you I loved you, I lied
I think you're stupid
I think we should use a condom
I think you should respect yourself more
I cheated on you, twice
Delete my number
Your broken heart is my greatest achievement
I pity you
Thank you
Goodbye
Don't go
No

Come back
I'm sorry
Good luck
I'm afraid
I miss you
I need you
I didn't mean it
I did it on purpose
When we got beaten up in Camden, I've never felt more alive
I always wished I grew up on an estate
I wish I were straight
I don't like to read
I wish I was white
I think most poetry is shit
I always wanted to be an emcee.

I Am Nobody's Nigger

Rappers, when you use the word 'nigger', remember
That's one of the last words Stephen Lawrence heard
So don't tell me it's a reclaimed word

I am nobody's nigger
So please, let my ancestors rest in peace
Not turn in their graves in Jamaican plantations
Or the watery graves of the slave trade
Thrown overboard into middle passage
Just for insurance claims
They were chained up on a boat
As many as they could manage and stay afloat
Stripped of dignity and all hope
Awaiting their masters and European names
But the sick and the injured were dead weight to toss
And Lloyd's of London would cover that cost

I am nobody's nigger
So you can tell Weezy and Drake
That they made a mistake
I am nobody's nigger now
So you can tell Kanye and Jigga
I am not a nigger . . . in Paris
I'm not a nigger in London
I'm not a nigger in New York

I'm not a nigger in Kingston
I'm not a nigger in Accra
Or a nigger with attitude in Compton
Cos 'I don't wanna be called yo nigga'

How were you raised on Public Enemy
And still became your own worst enemy?
You killed hip-hop and resurrected headless zombies
That can't think for themselves or see where they're going
Or quench the blood lust because there's no blood flowing
In their hearts, just in the streets
They don't give a damn as long as they eating
Their hearts ain't beating, they're cold as ice (bling)
Cos they would put money over everything
Money over self-respect or self-esteem
Or empowering the youth to follow their dreams
Stacking paper cos it's greater than love it seems
Call me 'nigger' cos you're scared of what 'brother' means

To know that we share something unspeakable
To know that as high as we rise we are not seen as equal
To know that racism is institutional thinking
And that 'nigger' is the last word you heard before a lynching.

Young, Black and Gay

My people are many and few
Subdivisions of me and you
Substantial people sometimes called subhuman
Negroes, faggots and all the youts dem
Don't think your rights came overnight
So many people had to fight
To gain anything like equality
We ain't there yet but we're gonna be

Institutions instigate internal indignation
We, brought up and betrayed by this nation
Isms and schisms of my Babylon home
Have held this king back from his throne
But you can fight the system from within
Yes you can befriend sinners and still not sin

See me, I went to university
Not even the first in my family
I'm from a long line of scholars
Trace me back to Greece and Africa
Through Cyprus and Jamaica
I don't write to be pretentious
But my vocab and vision leave you defenceless
Trying hard to avoid the clichés
But everything worth saying's been said these days

I'm ironic and yet I'm so on it
So if you wanna test me, let me hear your phonics
I'm not a battle emcee; I'm a community defender
Young, black and gay, you best remember.

Revolution

There is a revolution awaiting warriors
I recognise many righteous soldiers

I will fight with you or alone
Like the king I am reclaim my throne

Me nah wait for your recognition
Me jus fire upon you with verbal ammunition

Me, One, I speak for myself
And nobody else

Every one of you has a voice
To speak or not, it is your choice

But silence is not golden
Silence is the truth stolen

And stealing of the truth
Is exactly what dem do to the youts

Miseducation relative deprivation
Mislead young minds' motivation

Dealers, hustlers living bullet time

Their lives could end in the space of a rhyme

They get all the attention
While the good them get no mention

Young boys growing up with no direction
No protection on his erection

Sowing his seeds
But not fulfilling their needs

Young girls left to raise children alone
No job and kicked out of home

On the benefit system
Where you fill in forms and no one listens

Please listen up when I speak
How many homeless you seen this week?

Begging for change
I said begging for change

Don't just be a sympathiser
See through the mist, be a realiser

See what has been done
To brother, sister, daughter, son

The revolution a go come
The revolution begins with one

But one is much stronger
If he listens to those who've lived longer

Listen to the wisdom of the elders
Dem want fi tell you if you want to know

When's the last time you saw your grandma or grandfather
It's time to go

With an open mind and loving soul
As a community, as a whole

There's so much to be told
You think dem lost it cos dem got old

No, dem just stopped sharing
Cos you done stopped caring

If you are now prepared to hear
Revolution may begin this year

Go forth with what you have been told
Tell young girl she's worth more than gold

Tell young boy what a man's about

The truth nah whisper, the truth does shout

We are the revolution
We are the solution

We hold the key
And it begins with you and me

We are the revolution
We are the solution

We hold the key
And it begins with unity.

Fatherless Nation

We're living in a fatherless nation
Where dads up and leave without hesitation
The seeds are sown but the house ain't a home
Because the kids are left feeling alone

He is the void in my heart
He is the reason I cry
He is the wellspring of my pain
I used to wish he would die

He is the one who cheated me
He is the one who refused me
He is the one who rejected me
How could he want to lose me?

He is always in my thoughts
I think he not who he should be
He is nothing to me
Yet without him I never would be

When faced with my eventual confrontation
He made his final declaration
Though I'd played out this scenario a million times before
I'm still left with this wound, scabbed over but still sore

See, I could not ask for any more of a conclusive response
I had hoped to hear 'sorry' but it was not uttered once
A cold and calculated ruthless reply
Is what I got after years of asking why

This call was inevitable he had time to prepare some lies
I'm glad he could not see the tears fall from my eyes
As telecommunicated words impaled me one by one
He can imagine he was talking to a mature, grown-up son

Breaking an abandoned boy who prayed he would come
Back to fulfil a vital role in this boy's life and no longer run
Away from the most important job a man could ever boast
Does world no longer know what matters most?

To give life is natural; to take life is wrong
To nurture life that you create is what should be done
He does not believe in what people say he should be
He lives and dies by his mistakes except his biggest – me

It makes it worse when I'm told I'm just like he
In arrogance and creativity we have an affinity
Sharing something is better than having nothing at all
Still there are times when I wish he would visit or call

Watching the door 'til he comes home
Waiting for he to call me on the phone
Anticipating he will rescue me from feeling alone

Watching he leave me for the last time
Waiting for he like in a dole-cheque line
Anticipating approval from he will be mine

Watching the space where he never stood
It's like waiting for bad to convert to good
Anticipating that he one day could
Come back, though I doubt he ever should

The absence of he caused me so much pain
I could not bear to share his surname
I refuse to be the legacy of he
I'm what I managed to be, in spite of he

There are others like he and others like me
So let's not allow a looping history
Fathers, be there for your creations
Help rebuild the fatherless nations.

Therapy

This is not supposed to be therapy
I go to therapy on Wednesdays
Being on stage is my getaway
Or hitting the dancefloor on a Saturday
I try to stay home on Sundays
Cos if I'm lucky my mum makes Sunday lunch
Roast chicken and potatoes, rice and peas
'And, Mummy? Don't forget the plantain!'
Yes, I know, she spoils me

I'm supposed to be happy
Because most would be if they were this lucky
I'm supposed to be the one 'living his dreams'
The one that they envy and aspire be like
I'm supposed to inspire but I cry out
I'm supposed to give hope but I'm so full of doubt

I'm supposed to know exactly what I'm doing
And precisely where I'm going
Because I am a leader . . . right?

I'm supposed to have the answer
Or at least ask the right questions
I'm supposed to be cruising in the fast lane
But I feel so pedestrian

He gave me this notebook to write in
I'm not supposed to tell anyone
But fuck what I'm supposed to do

I've always done what I'm supposed to
I was supposed to get my GCSEs, A Levels and a degree
Check one, check two and, yes, check three
A whole bunch of Bs and Cs and a 2:1 in my degree
English and Philosophy
What else was I equipped to be but some kind of writer
Well I'm pretty good with kids, I coulda been a teacher
But even my favourite at school, Mr Rattigan, told me
'Never . . . ! Ever . . . ! Become a teacher. You can do more.'

My granddad always asks me
'When are you gonna go back to your studies?'
He tells our family back in Cyprus that I'm a professor
Dr Dean Atta
But I'm far from a doctor
My only PhD a Player Hating Degree
But I don't stay put long enough for you to hate on me
Supposedly
I'm a poet slash playwright slash producer
Slash artistic associate slash creative director
Slash confused dot com
Online searching for my ID
On Facebook faking familiarity
Retweeting at you hashtag complete me

BBM me, B-befriend me
This iPhone is not my phone it's a loan of identity
See, I can be whatever and whoever I want to be
With the right accessory, by any app necessary

I'm supposed to be grateful for all this freedom
Free to grab opportunities when I see them
Because some let things pass them by
Fixated on money
Trapped by responsibility
Or bound by their apathy
'Our deepest fear is not that we are inadequate.
Our deepest fear is that we are powerful beyond imagination.'
I believed that first time I heard it and I
Still do
But am I supposed to be afraid?
Cos I'm not

I don't need words from page to reach out and hug me
Comfort me or tell me that they love me
I just need them to tell the truth
Cos I'm supposed to be here
And I'm supposed to do this
And, no, this isn't therapy
But it sure feels good to me
To be sharing this, with you.

Paper Cuts

I write for forgiveness
Forgiveness of my apathy
I write for understanding
Understanding of myself
I write about me, mostly
Mostly I write for nothing
But sometimes I write for money

I write for recognition
My poetry is a protest
Just because I don't march
Doesn't mean I don't care
I can write in solidarity
I don't have to be there, on the street
When a million men march on a beat
I stand a capella, on my own two feet
I can speak against injustice
From a stage or on the page
I'm a poet not a politician
But I canvas for your vote
With these words I wrote
My ballot box is my bank account
Your voting slips are in your wallet

I write to leave a legacy but I am no myth
And I rarely write with any idea in mind
Of how my words will change the world
But I like to think they will

The pen is mightier than
Any paper it writes upon
I could literally rewrite history
But you can't prove a thing
With a page left blank
Are these words worth more on the page?
Yes, if no one is listening

If a writer writes alone who hears her pen?
Just her, but all could read her story
If she shouts out alone who hears her then?
Just her, but at least she feels better
But if no one knows her story
Who could say she was alive?
When you die, do you know what will survive?
Do you trust and treasure your memories most?
Do you haunt your yesterday like a living ghost?

I write to my ego, a black hole to validation
I could write books on behalf of this nation
And archive them to be discovered as truth
Such is the vanity of my youth

But what if we had to write in blood?
If we could no longer write out our own
Secret solitary hypothetical revolutions
If all words were inextricably linked to their maker
Would you stamp your own DNA on what you say?
Write in haemoglobin like hieroglyphics on a wall?
If red ink were all that we had
If we had to suffer for our voice
If to bleed were the only choice
I would bleed slowly and measured
My every word would be treasured
I would not write for my leisure or pleasure

I did not bleed for this poem
But I could not help but pour
My whole heart and my soul
Into these words

This world has seen enough
Blood shed
To leave every page soaked
Blood red
So maybe we could use our
Paper as bandages, instead.

I Am Red

I am tired eyes
Teenage highs
The evidence I've cried
Robin with no Batman
A sidekick with no hero
My own worst enemy
I am in love with my weakness
Charging towards the matador cape of my own downfall
I am red today
¡Olé!
Mad at myself
I am simmering
I am seething
Am I bleeding?
Innocence bludgeoned
Roses are . . . not for you
I am the thorn waiting for you to pick what I protect
I am The Passion: The Sequel
Second-hand stigmata
I am here in vein
A pound of flesh
I am a red letter
I am an unread letter
The debt and the debtor
I am red tape

I am a velvet rope with no admission
I am waiting for permission
Rehearsing on stage with no audition
I am red curtains with no one to lift them
I am a work of fiction
Red Riding Hood
With no hood, no woods, no basket full of goods
I am the axe that cut myself open
Both hunter and hunted
Heartbreaker and heartbroken
I am words unspoken
I am the fairy tale
And the harsh reality
We all make mistakes
Just look at me
Circled, crossed out, underlined
I am a stop sign
Next to a double red line
Undermined
Denied
Boarding the bus with no fare
Posting myself with no stamp
Phoning home with no change
Red nose day with no comedy
I am red in the face
Caught red-handed
I am doing the time
The digital display of an alarm clock

Facebook notifications on your phone
Flagged emails RE:
Important
Urgent
Reply ASAP
Drop everything
Deal with me
Stop what you're doing
Help me
Look at me
Look at me now
Not in a minute
Not in an hour
Not tomorrow
Now
I am red right now
Bathing in blood
Drowning in wine
Smashing through every stop sign
But when you finally ask me how I am
I'll tell you, 'I'm fine.'

New Year

New ideas here
New hopes, new dreams
From which I awake
My body starts to shake
Sending a vibration
Through this nation
I seem cold
They seem old
Those resolutions, rehashed and reheated
Returned from last year, partially defeated
Hopefully committed to, hopefully, this time
Held aloft by you but exposed by this rhyme

You take the easy way out
You are so proud about
Your once-a-year success
Earth rotates in distress
A smoke signal ascends
To universal friends
For some sort of solution
To this state of revulsion
I feel repulsion yet I feel liable
If we're not aiding we're adding to it
That is undeniable

Once more you fake it like a whore
What you call charity has already been paid for
In blood, sweat and tears
Over hundreds of years
New year, new ideas here
Take a new stance, a new view
This is a new chance for a new you.

Ascension

I rise, I have risen, and yet I feel like

I'm falling

Falling from grace

Falling short of my potential

Falling out of favour with those who expected, predicted
Were counting on so much for me and my future

If this is the future, take me back to the past
When I had hopes, dreams and ambitions
And not just debts, regrets and not quite yets
When a blank page offered up infinite possibilities
Not just a potential paycheck
And an escape from a job where I get no respect
And yet, I rise to positions of responsibility
And accountability
I rise to capitalist desires
Not at school waiting for playtime
But at work waiting for payday
Daydreaming of a play date
Where butterflies would lift off from a pit of acid
Rise and make noise in the form of words

Strung together as a puppeteer connects to a puppet

I rise to the occasion
I have been cocooned too long
My flight is imminent
I boil over in a storm
And though torrential rain may descend upon me
The same water that sustains my being and form
I rise above and beyond
Standing on the wings of the butterflies
And treading the raindrops
Like a stairway to Heaven
And so although they fall – I rise
Like the towers that scrape the skies
Though oxygen is thin up here
I stand tall while others crawl and gasp for breath
I breathe the air of the gods
Filled with stardust and plane emissions
I don't need an engine for my ascension

I rise from sleep and depression
And found all other psychological conditions remained
And within a system of liars the truth seems like insanity
So how do I defy gravity?

I rise free from my former inhibitions to realise
The only opinions that matter to me
Are that of God and my mother

See a clear destination and a strong foundation
Won't stop precipitation
But when you understand the cycle
You don't fear it any more than a river fears evaporation
The sea has been in the sky so why can't I?

I rise, I fall, and through it all
I learn to linger a little higher.

Freedom of Love
after André Breton

My mother who spoils me
My mother who let me stay rent-free
My mother who texts me on her lunch break
To see if I'll be home for dinner
My mother is a giver
My mother has given her life to my sister and I
My mother couldn't be selfish even if she tried
My mother has been a mother from the age of eighteen
My mother is searching for her own identity
My mother remains optimistic in the face of redundancy
My mother cares not for money
If the mortgage is covered and our basic needs are met
My mother isn't used to luxury
Maybe a manicure but not much more
My mother used to sing in our church choir
My mother loves to sing around the house
My mother sings the wrong lyrics
Even after you tell her the right ones
My mother makes big meals in a small kitchen
My mother does more than make do
She makes miracles look effortless
My mother is single and successful
My mother is not alone, but lonely sometimes
My mother is loved and respected and admired

My mother is tired
My mother is more than poetry
She is the breath before we speak
My mother is not impressed by words alone.

Mother Tongue

Our mother has swallowed her tongue
Though selfish is never a word I could call Mum
I feel she has been so by swallowing her tongue

To make it worse
Our family holidays
Are always to her motherland
She forgets to translate
Even though she knows
We don't understand
My sister and I
Make do and get by
On the meaning we can infer
From gestures and inflection
Can never look to Mum for direction
Mother has swallowed her tongue
Shows no regrets on reflection
Stubborn. She refuses to see
That she has wronged us not to teach
To give us the option, the basic right
Of freedom of speech
With our grandparents
Our aunts, uncles and our cousins

There are few shortcuts to understanding
Common language is a good paving stone
So when you can't speak the language of love
You realise you may be walking this path alone
Made in England, we're half this and half that
But they could more easily overlook that fact
If we could speak with our mother's tongue
Not let our skin speak for us
But join in the family chorus
I can't tell you why
She would wilfully deny
Her daughter and her son
But she has swallowed it
And we are struck dumb
Our mother has swallowed her tongue.

The Flamingo

As I fled the midday
Sun, that only tourists
Would venture out in
I found a cool shelter
In the municipal gallery
On the seafront

There I saw the sculpture
Of that flamingo
With large wings
In the shape of the island
Bound horizontally, north of centre, with a red string

What instantly
Became apparent to me
Was the need for art
To explain feelings
Where words would fail

In this common
Visual, visceral, language
This work of art
Would need no translation
Either side of the divide

I wasn't there for the war
But in that moment I saw
And, in my way, understood
What this border meant
For Cyprus – the flamingo
Who could no longer fly.

Smash and Grab

It was a blazing hot night in London
I wasn't there. I was in Larnaca, Cyprus
At my second home with my family
Mum, sister and my yiayia and bapou
(That means grandparents in Greek
A language that I can barely speak)
I try to understand the news in Greek
Most words beyond my comprehension

But those images spoke for themselves
A death. A protest. Rioting. Looting. Fires
A few long-distance phone calls and texts
To check my nearest and dearest at home
And to get a clearer understanding
Of how this all started and how it might end
From a distance it looked quite exciting
Masked youths and riot police fighting

From a distance I didn't think about houses
Family businesses and innocent passersby
Having turned off our international roaming
We knew nothing of plans on BB Messenger
To replicate these riots, to copycat this chaos
To duplicate the destruction, to loot high streets
Across capital and country . . . From a distance

It just looked like a hot night in London

Hot tempers flared by unanswered
Questions. Violent cries to police silence
Arson and greed. Protest impersonators walking
Home with flat screen TVs, to be mounted
On their walls like trophies or sold instead
What a way to disrespect the dead
At that point I felt so sorry for Mark's family
Whose personal protest had been hijacked

Then further news stories of Syria and Somalia
Make Londoners look like spoilt children
'What do we want?' 'Everything!'
'When do we want it?' 'Now!'
We have raised these children. We can't just blame
The parents, social media, the police or politicians
In a way, I was glad to see our young people realised
Their power that hot night, even if only in destruction

With such inflation on an education what can you expect
But ignorant behaviour from those who cannot afford it?
But my university degree gives me
No better understanding right now
It's no wonder no one looted the libraries
They wanted trainers so they could run
From you and your bullets, made of metal
Rubber and discriminatory legislation

Forget about future aspirations; not waiting
For 2012 to go for gold but a smash and grab
Relay. Jack the jewellery shop then down
To Dixons so they could watch their own
Instant replay on HD widescreen plasma TV
But why do these children hate a country
That so many would literally die to get to?

Seeking asylum and refuge, running
From war and persecution to us
Where we ignore and we pretend
Are politically correct and politically inept
Do nothing about anything we can possibly
Avoid or sweep under the rug
As a carpet of crime covers this country
What's truly criminal is the neglect
With which we have raised these children.

Mr Invincible

What you looking at?
Don't you know who I am?

Well you best get to know fools
Because I am the man

Mr Invincible, Mr Unstoppable
I'm above that, below that

(Whatever yeah, I'm just not with that)
Don't tell me where to go

Don't tell me what to do
Don't tell me what I know

I may know nothing of value to you
But I know what I need

To survive in this world, this world of greed
That's what I'm doing, surviving; you can't call this living

I have tried to change but of my past you are unforgiving
I'm what you all call delinquent, disaffected

All your norms and values I've rejected
Where are these doors of opportunity?

Opportunity? For you, maybe, not for me
I see all them doors are held shut from behind

But I don't mind, nah, I don't mind
Because I'm Mr Invincible, Mr Unstoppable

Mr Dead before my time but at least I died beautiful

I want to live a good life but this world won't let me
I only big myself up because I'm scared you'll forget me

Or hurt me or leave me or cheat and deceive me
You can't count on anyone in this world, believe me

All I want is some love but here I am, loveless
No one holds out a hand because they think I'm hopeless

If people are commodities consider me surplus
Not wanted because of what they see on the surface

I may look thugged-out but really I'm full of doubt
I go on all gangsterfied but inside I'm petrified

I thought I was invincible. One bullet. I died.

Key to the City

Your minds are the lock
And my words are the key
Fitting to open you up
With a little story
About this boy named John
He's on the streets of your ends
It don't matter where he came from
He ain't got the key to the city
He ain't even got the key to a front door
He thought London would be pretty
But he soon found out it was raw
He's run away from a broken home
And the care system.
He's been gone six months
And still no one has missed him
The only friend he ever had
Was this girl named Melissa
Everywhere he goes
He carries her picture
She was like his sister
His mother, his lover
And when he kissed her
She was his world
But then she got fostered
And left the children's home

The staff told him to forget her
Let her go, leave her alone
They told him that her location
Was confidential information
He wrote letters to be passed on
But they never reached their destination
All he knew was that she went to London
So he decided to follow
When he landed, he found himself stranded
With nowhere to go
His passion and hasty decision
Turned into months of regret and sorrow
His lost love pained him like a sickness
So he sought out street pharmacists
He quickly became addicted
But found no fix as good
As his love's sweet kiss

John approached me
At the bus stop
Just last week
I admit, I judged him
Before he even started to speak

He said, 'Give me some money.'
And I said, 'No, I know where that money's gonna go.'
He said, 'Please, bruv, I'm hungry.'
I said, 'I'll buy you a sandwich then.'

He said, 'I don't want that.'
I said, 'I'll get you some chicken and chips.'
He said, 'Nah, I'm a vegetarian.'
I said, 'Well, then I'll buy you a salad.'
He said, 'Look, I just want the money, yeah, I just want the money.'
I said, 'Well, I just want many things but beggars can't be choosers.'
He said, 'I ain't a beggar, bruv, I ain't a beggar.'
I said, 'Well, then I beg you, bruv, just move on.'

And that was the last I ever saw of John
But I thought about him all day long
I felt a bit ashamed
And a little bit guilty
But mostly I felt lucky
Because although I ain't got the key to the city
I got keys to houses in Wembley, Stonebridge
Harlesden and Cyprus
From north-west London
To the Mediterranean
Wherever I lay my hat
That's my home
I've been to Paris, Amsterdam
Barcelona, Egypt
And it's all the same
Just people on a hustle
Locked in the city mind-state

Businessmen
And men in the business
Of making a profit at all costs
Career women
And women whose careers
Are taking all their clothes off
School kids
And kids getting schooled by the streets
Used by the streets, abused by the streets
Confused by these streets
And their portrayal in music and on TV
See me I'm from North Weezy
But I'm not on Channel U reppin' ends
And I don't roll with a crew
Just a few close friends.
I make moves on my Oyster card
I don't drive a Benz
I've got ten pounds in my pocket
Until the week ends
I speak on Facebook
Because T-Mobile locked off my phone
My friends come check me still
I am never alone
But this city can be lonely
That's why youths roll with crews
And this city can be dangerous
That's why many carry tools
See all they want is comfort and protection

But all they get is stigma and rejection
Then they get locked up
For one stupid mistake
And they're caught in a cycle
So hard to break
Either in and out of prison
Or on and off the junk
Or both in many cases
And John, he's well on his way
His story is one of many
Misguided youths and runaways
See John went on to get some money
Later on that night
He jumped a girl in an alley
Taking advantage of the lack of light
He grabbed her from behind
And put a knife to her neck
He had not done this before
He was a desperate and nervous wreck
He told her not to move
But for some reason
She tried to turn around
His knife ran her though
And he dropped her
Face down on the ground
John took her purse
Bought his medicine
And forgot the whole day

While his lost love Melissa
Lay bleeding in an alleyway.

Without You

My achievements
Don't seem to matter
The bubbles in this champagne
Seem flatter than water

I was wishing on a star
And I can't believe I caught her
Then let her go

My hands are far from empty though
The illuminations are plentiful

I see constellations full of imitations

Temporarily, I'm blinded by the lights
But none shine as bright as you

In '04 when you first came into view
I knew you were one of a kind
I loved you more
Than any one of my rhymes
Love so true
I doubt I could ever find it again

My best friend
I knew I was blessed when
We would share a bed at night
Or just talk for hours on the phone

With you in my life I never felt alone
But now lonely is the only other company
Even though I'm living quite comfortably

There is no one I can tell how I truly feel
So call me 'Shh . . .' cos my lips are sealed

When I was lost
You were the one who found me

When I was confused
You spoke those harsh truths

When I was a mess
To you I could confess

When I lost hope
You kept me afloat

Now
'As two ships passing in the night
So quietly neath the stars soft light
Our paths cross but now and then'

But it will ever feel the same again
You ascend, as you dream
With your eyes wide open

I'm still wishing on a star
When the dawn has broken

Without you.

Shadow Boxer

Oscar Wilde said, 'Be yourself
Everyone else is taken'
But if I found your life vacant
I might take it
Because I believe
I would make the better you

But who's to tell?

Who was the better Batman
Better Bond or Doctor Who?

Like you're Smallville
And I'm Superman 2
The prequel to my sequel
My not quite déjà vu

I walk in scuffed shoes
That are new to you
Speak in tired clichés
That are news to you

I look at my reflection
And I see you
An instant vintage kind of guy

A J Dilla kind of Blue Note
Revisited – with new hope

Yours is a heart that only just broke
A mouth that only speaks the truth

After the gold rush of your youth
Will come a time to harvest dreams
But you journey through the past
Trying to make each moment last

Time fades away
But your visions of love
Are here to stay

If I woke up wearing your T-shirt
Would I feel the same way?

Would I miss my own four letters
Or embrace your name?

Would I know the names
Of more super heroes?

Would I know more about
70s west-coast folk or
80s and 90s hip-hop?

Would my talent grow?

Would my confidence drop?

If I could see through your eyes
Maybe I would know why
You could not walk away
From the games she played

Cos when your shadow boxes back
You can't bob and weave that for long

When you've shared a bed with kryptonite
No wonder you feel weak at night
Wear a costume and pretend it's all right
The Joker dressed up as the Dark Knight

The spy with no mission
Just sharp suits and women
Drinking scotch on the rocks
Looking suave with no money
And no clue
Of just how awesome you are

I look at my reflection
And I see you
Standing there, next to me
And it's the perfect view.

Ego Extensions

If you treat
Other people
Like extensions
Of your ego

And don't see
Them as complete
And independent
Of you

Unspoken
Assumptions
Will hurt more
Than the truth

That no one
Was put
On this earth
Just for you.

More Than This

I knew, before we'd even spoken
My skinny-jean-clad punk-rock poet
Tattooed and pierced
Painted and punctured
Denim, metal and ink
Pint glass in one hand
Poem in the other
Mouthfuls of beer dislodge illicit imagery
And forbidden metaphors
Crumpled A4 sheet casually discarded
As the last lyrics leave his lips

He leaves me naked
On a tobacco and cannabis speckled rug
On his living-room floor
Wrapped up in a blanket, damp with semen, lubricant
And the cold tea we spilled in our frantic lovemaking
'I've got to go to work,' he says, 'You can let yourself out.'

I guess it's nice to know I can get what I want
But maybe I should want more than this.

Off the Wall

I know exactly the order these records will play
Still I hope the DJ will surprise me today
They say you can't meet a king in a club
But you were quite the Prince Charming
Disarming me from the get-go
I let go of all my inhibitions
Took my back off the wall and accepted your invitation
Most guys in here I wouldn't give a second glance
But there was something about your bold advance
That convinced me to take this chance and dance

Pause

Sorry, I'm already telling lies
I'm a wolf in a fluffy disguise
I'm no shrinking violet wallflower
But I'd like to let you think I'm shy
I'm not so unobtainable
I pretend to be unapproachable
In the hope that you'll approach me
I notice you noticing me
Ignore you purposefully
And wait here patiently
Seemingly aloof

Now you know the truth
Do you think I'm a player?
Desperate? Deluded or just damaged?
Can you tell me? Cos I can't be certain
All I know is I'm here constantly hurting
I thought the pain would fade with a little harmless flirting
But their eyes cut across me like these disco laser lights
They say when you die your life flashes before your eyes
Then I guess I've been dying to meet you here
Because I see my dating history all around us

Rewind

An early ex-boyfriend who still calls me most days
I'm still his go-to guy even though I make him cry
When we have sex we say, 'I love you' – a true lie

Then there's the sweetest guy I ever met
Who I strung along for a couple of months
Before saying, 'Let's just be friends'

That guy with whom I had
The World's Greatest First Date Ever
But he never called again

And then a former friend I fell out with
Not long after falling into bed with

And that guy I kissed one, two, many times
And have no regrets about
Even though we both had partners at the time

I can't stop
I won't stop
I don't stop
Even though I get more than enough

I Can't Help It; It's the Falling In Love
With the idea of falling in love
When I Get On The Floor and Rock With You

'You' being the man who stands before me now
Or last week
Or last year
Is the picture becoming clear?

If you knew all this, would you still take my hand
And lead me past them past men on to the dancefloor?

Fast forward

And the records spin; we are one hour in
But it's pretty clear you are not my king
I don't have the desire to dance all night
Not to say I don't admire yours
We don't have the connection I hoped we might

Not to say I think you're flawed
We are all imperfect
Our imperfection can make this selection easy or hard
Depending on how and where you have been scarred
Beaten, bruised, torn apart and left in Love's mortuary
I've had my fair share of wear and tear
I have torn, bruised and broken others
(But I only kill the connection
I don't literally murder lovers)
They're not skeletons in my closet
This isn't murder on the dancefloor
But we are grooving in a graveyard
Rocking and rolling in the rubble of relationships
Lost lust, mistrust
Where I see all of this
You see only us

Stop

This was just a game from the beginning
But neither of us is any closer to winning
This record is all played out
This club, a coliseum of carnal catastrophe
It's not the soundtrack or the sodomy that bothers me
It's my growing lack of empathy
And the always leaving here feeling empty
And the always coming back wanting more
Of what is not on offer

They say you can't meet a king in a club
That's why this king will wear no crown
Until they burn this disco down.

My Love
after Joshua Idehen

My love is amnesia
Never knowing its home
It met you in a club
And dumped you by poem
My love rhymes with everything
It can't have been a could've been
If it should've been, it would've been
It can't be seen through green eyes
It's not surprising that you found a new love
It publicly denies ever loving you
But it doesn't die; it regenerates
In a blue police 'public call' box
A disguise; larger on the inside
My love has no telephone
If it could travel through time
It would love itself through history
My love is no great mystery
It's a glass half empty
Amaretto on the rocks
A friendly drunk
Makes love wearing socks
And gets cold feet wearing your shoes
'And I will always love you'
Is not something it would say

My love is this; the fifth fucking draft
Of a poem trying to describe my love

It would never make a mix tape
It abandons every Rubik's Cube
It is not retro nor is it cool
My love is a special kind of fool
It hates hotel rooms without holidays
And perfect partners who live far away
It's definitely not 'What's Good?'
My love is not misunderstood
But it could never 'Say it Right'
It is a boxer who doesn't fight
It would never date a comedian
It doesn't laugh at or tell jokes
It snorts coke with drag queens
Smokes weed with waste men
It has dreams but would never chase them
A Christmas present in June
Either too late or far too soon
A gift that I'd never give
A ghost who's never lived
And never known closure
Because it never begins the right way
My love is amnesia
Never knowing its home
It met you in a club
And dumped you by poem

My love is frightfully familiar
But you would never know
It doesn't know what it could be
Because I am afraid to show it.

Rome is Eternal

She said that road was closed
When a car fell through the pavement
Because everyone here knows
Rome is built on many layers

Streets on top of streets, centuries deep
I was half-listening to her but I was also
Checking out a guy in tightly fitting jeans
She said, 'He's not gay, he's just Italian.'

Those telltale signs don't translate here
Even body language was foreign to me
Back home I can suss men out speedily
With successful subtlety but here in Rome

My gaydar flashed left right everywhere
With many layers of miscommunication
So I turned to my trusty iPhone
For some serious investigation

I log on to Grindr; iPhone gay sex finder
Yep, 'there's an app for that'
I didn't come to Rome for this
Random sex isn't something that I miss

Almost a year without a one-night stand
This certainly wasn't planned
But it was a welcome surprise
When he popped up on my iPhone screen

(Location 24 metres away)

My friend who grew up here said
She didn't know anyone who was gay
Yet for two years this hot gay man
Has lived in the apartment above her

So I guess this guy knows how to
Keep his business undercover
But then came me and my poetry
Shamelessly, I expose late-night iniquity

While my friend slept, up the stairs
I crept to meet this man of mystery
If you'd asked before, I'd've said for sure
My days of sleeping around were history

But as he opened his apartment door, what I saw
In his wise eyes made me feel differently
How did I feel such heat for a complete stranger?
At 2 a.m. we meet, discreetly, and I feel no danger

We were smoking a spliff and listening to Radiohead
Next thing we were kissing and I was giving him ____
We had instant rapport, I felt so relaxed
There's nothing I'd change if I could go back

And when he said he was coming to London
Clapham to be precise, my first thought was
To déjà vu this rendezvous would be nice
To walk on pavements cars don't fall through

To speak loud and public with body language
But then I thought of why I had done this
And what I wanted to achieve. I had nothing
More to give and nothing I wanted to receive

From this ancient city where new technology
Found a tender moment in close proximity
Because now this night is eternal like Rome
And in this poem I can take Leonardo home.

How Did We

It started, as these things do, with a kiss
And we saw it as just some harmless fun
And though in the moment it feels like bliss
We feel so awkward when the deed is done

As soon as I come I'm ready to go
As soon as I leave I want to return
You're my kryptonite; I just can't say no
You're that lesson I never seem to learn

Every exit is a revolving door
Every question is answered with a kiss
Every warning sign I choose to ignore
Cos if you're so wrong why did I write this?

Why when you're near can I not think clear
I keep asking myself how did we get here?

Matters of the Heart

Clutched our phones tightly
When we could not hold on
To each other

We burned minutes
To make up for the distance
We gazed into space

Between letters
Carefully crafted
Text messages

Misunderstood attempts
To mind the gap between
What was heard and said

Written and read
Consonants and vowels
Words and sounds

Don't touch me the way I need you to
I can paint pretty pictures
With poetry

But words are not enough
When it comes to matters
Of the heart.

Fragmented

When I wake in the morning
To the warmth of your skin
I know I need you
At least I want to need you

Don't say that you love me
I can't bear to deceive you
A fragmented heart inside
To fix it – many have tried

To tear my chest open
Ran and left it broken
I am remade of superglue
That is why I stick to you.

Quit Me

If you gave yourself a deadline
To quit, it wouldn't make it any
Easier for you. So you should
Just cut me off right now or else

You'll abuse your dependence
On me until the very last day of
Your futile countdown. Your
Lips will miss me softly pressed

Against them. Your body will
Yearn for me to course my way
Inside you. You'll reach out for
Me and then someone will

Remind you that you said that
You don't want me, in fact you
Resent me, and then your whole
Day will seem pointless and

Empty. Without me, as your fix
In the morning, at lunch, after
Work and for comfort and
Counsel last thing at night

You say I help you to relax; I
Ease your mind. You open up
With me because I put a
Welcome haze over reality

Albeit momentarily, I help you
To cope with this so-called life
Where you're misunderstood
And things go bad when all you

Try to do is good. I know you
Over-exaggerate and I indulge
You and that's the worst thing
That I can possibly do. And

When you cannot have me
You'll take it out on your
Friends and family. You'll
Break down when you see

Another with me. I wasn't
Trying to trap you in this
Habitual cycle I just came to
Offer you relief and now you

Think I'm your only hope of
Happiness. And I'm the only
One you turn to in times of

Stress and grief. Your life was

Rich and full before me and it
Can be again. You're stronger
Than this, you can do it now if

You done did it then. Because
The good I do for you is not
Good enough, if I daily infect
You and cause you pain. See

You've been warned against me
You've heard the stories – but
You take this risk because you
Think I'm worth it. You think

That you're informed and you
Truly know me. But if you only
Knew how much I could hurt
You, you'd think twice before

You reached out for me.

Tunnel Vision

Forget lights, tunnels, silver linings
I want time travel and you

They say there's a better man for me
And I'll find him

But I don't want someone new
Forget my tears and forget yours

Forget my fears and closing train doors
Forget hotel rooms

And gone too soons
Been so longs

Poems and love songs
Forget all my words

Yes even this verse
And meet me again

And kiss me
Like the first time

I can't see light at the end of this tunnel
If you stand there with him.

Enough

The world is not enough
The sun, the moon, the stars
You said time is all it takes
You said the universe was ours

Tonight is not enough
I want you yesterday and tomorrow
Yet one of those is impossible
And that's my greatest sorrow

The truth is not enough
When liars reign supreme
When hearts have bled out
Children don't dare to dream

Dreams are not enough
To fill the void in my soul
The beat beneath my breast
Collapsed into a black hole

The world is not enough
The sun, the moon, the stars
You devour hearts and dreams
You said the universe was ours.

Ghostwriter

I'm feeling you
Way more than you would want me to
Do anything you want me to
Ask me, I'd wear bombs for you
This is more than vulnerable
It's volatile
Uncomfortable
This situation the negation
Of Independence Day

Fireworks in the sky
Not the 4th of July
But the 5th of November
I am a Guy Fawkes effigy
It burns me to remember, remember
Our dates in September
October
November
December

Your cold heart froze my petals
Unable to bloom, frostbitten
I cling to you

I should let go
And be glad for what we had
For the memories of you
Feeling me, feeling you
Misleading and deceiving you
Is what I do when I smile
It hurts me too much to describe

I have died
I am a ghost to you
What am I supposed to do?
Write for you?
Fight for you?

I'm a headless horseman
Riding into the night for you
Holding out a torch of black light for you
See me not
I do not want you to
Fear me not
I am no harm to you
Hear me not
These words are not for you
These words are not for you.

Missing Persons

You evade the page
Not a room I can lock nor a door I can close
Empty doorframe, missing windowpane
In between lines, beyond margins
Parts of a story one might skip
Look past, not notice
Something remains
Unsaid.

Severance

The boy I let go
Dropped
Broke off
Up some break
I break down
Amputee me
These stumps
Cannot stretch
Round a thousand plus yesterdays
My interest in
This time past
Does not make up for my absence
I could've been there
Were it not for pride
Mine and yours
But mostly mine
I am not the man you knew
When you knew me
I was bleeding
So many red hands
None of them the real culprit
I was the one
Doing the lashing
Whipping myself
With my past

Cutting myself
Off
From my present
By hacking
Hacking at
Whatever wouldn't
Fit
Down a narrow path
I saw for my future
Self-inflicted
Severance
From parts
Of my self
Now stumps
Of memory
A right hand
My best foot
That went forward
And re-rooted themselves
Appearing to forget

              the violence

                     of our separation

You say I'm gentle
You say my words are gentle
Losing limbs
Is a painful thing
With my tongue
I lick my wounds.

Second Hand

It was not because I wanted time
To rewind, stand still or speed up

It was not because I hoped it would
Bring forgiveness or take away hurt

It was not because I had dreamed
About this for many months now

It was not because we were alone
It was not because I had the perfect

Opportunity, the perfect evening
And the perfect image of myself

Reflected in your too familiar eyes
It was not because your eyes still

Looked so somber after all those years
Not because your stories still

Evoked sympathy after all those years
Not because I felt guilty still

And responsible after all those years
It was not because I was a man then

And you were in your teenage years
I was not concerned about how we

Remembered, sounded or appeared
It was because it felt right, so right

And yet filled me with insecurities
I'd not felt since my teenage years

I had not feared kissing another man
Privately, in well over eight years

It was not because I felt any shame
It was not because I felt any blame

No more than I had when I saw you before
A year ago when you accepted my apology

We had put it all behind us
It was not what was behind us

It was what was in front of me
It was the most beautiful man

It was the most beautiful man
I had ever seen, in front of me

You are still the most beautiful
Man I have ever seen

You are still my one regret
But you were not the loss to me

And you were not all lost to me
You were there, in bed with me

But I was too afraid to kiss you
It was not because I wanted time

To rewind, stand still or speed up
But because I wanted the hands

Of time to hold me. Hold me like
I should have held onto you then

Hold me and carry me forward
Because there is no going back

My arms, like the clock I watch
As they reach out and they wait

For a second hand to catch them up
But the second hand will never stop

Be it ahead or just behind,
Always at the right time.

Lost in Time

Lost in time is Woolworths
Live & Kicking, *SMTV Live*
Nokia 3210s and Snake
Lost in time are my tap shoes
And singing lessons with Ray
Lost in time is the bouncy castle
At my birthday party, aged six
Lost in time are my milk teeth
The Tooth Fairy, Father Christmas
The Easter Bunny
And Teenage Mutant Hero Turtles
Lost in time are Opal Fruits
And Marathon bars
Lost in time are my first pair
Of Clarks shoes, my youth
The truth
Lost in time is an excuse
Lost in time is regret
Memory, heartache, skin
Lost in time is her waistline
His mind, her confidence, his money
Lost in time are my grandmother's dreams
My father's ambitions and my cousin's name
Lost in time is that incident on the Southbank
After which we were never the same

Lost in time is the opportunity
To make it up to you
The healing my mother advised us to do
The mutual friends
To plait together our loose ends
Lost in time are my dreadlocks
My university days, philosophy essays
One-pound pints
One-night stands
Tripping on magic mushrooms
And free raves in the woods
Lost in time is calling Brighton home
Lost in time is my grandparents'
House in Harlesden
Lost in time is being afraid
To visit family in Jamaica
Lost in time is my gaydar.com profile
Adam4adam, gayromeo and blackgaychat
Lost in time are nights spent
In Heaven and Bootylicious
Lost in time is meeting you
At Lyric Hammersmith
And watching you perform
At Hampstead Theatre
The performance I didn't do
At Theatre Royal Stratford East
Because I couldn't go on stage and pretend
Lost in time is performing

Other people's words on stage
My fear of a blank page
And my phase of prolific writing
Lost in time is the new and exciting
Discovery of another man's body
Lost in time is running
My fingers through your hair
Lost in time is virginity
The perfect moment
Silence, patience, innocence
Lost in time is the evening
You introduced me to your family
Lost in time is your father's respect for me
Lost in time is me giving you
Travel money to come see me
Lost in time is your love for me
Lost in time is the man
Who feels worthy of your love
Lost in time are your hands in mine
Heart beating double time at your touch
Lost in time is when I was ill
And you sat by my bedside
Lost in time is when you cycled to my house
To hand-deliver me a poem
And even though I was home
You simply posted it through the letterbox
You didn't knock
Lost in time is wondering why

These tears I cry
Denying my flaws
Obsessing over past mistakes
Crippling doubt and depression
Lost in time is worrying
About being a gay Christian
And any doubt
That 'God Is Good – All The Time!'
Lost in time is worrying
About being predictable
Lost in time is worrying
About repeating myself
Lost in time is Woolworths
Live & Kicking, *SMTV Live*
Nokia 3210s and Snake.

Poems

I send envelopes of hope
Addressed to our tomorrow
I don't want to write poems
I want to scribble appreciative notes
On whatever I can find
Wish-you-were-here rectangles
When you're not by my side
We-need-this lists
Of things for you to buy
Love letters, emails and texts
Words you will never forget
'Good morning'
On a steamy bathroom mirror
Birthday cards
Not trying to make up for my absence
From the rest of your year
I don't want to write words that cut like paper
Sting but barely bleed
I don't want to write my needs
Just yours and mine combined
I don't want to write poems about you
I want to write a dedication to you
In my first published poetry collection
I want to write you promises in permanent marker
To feel real human shame if I forsake these words

I will make these words come true through you
Not by ink but with lips and tongue
Fingertips and hips
Buttocks and biceps
Feet and talcum-powdered toes
Eager earlobes
Praying palms
Forearms and forehead
One hand gripping your hair
The other stroking your chin
Hot breath on every inch of skin
I don't want to write poems
I want to write fascinating contradictions
Not flash fiction to fulfil a literary addiction
Chasing lines into sleepless nights
Eyelids shut to reveal tattoos of you within
I don't want to write, 'Forgive him'
Or scrawl an invitation into sin
I don't want to build biro bridges between you and I
I don't want to write us walking off into the sunset
Don't want to blot the sunrise from your eyes
Younger teacher
Student no longer
I don't want to force revision
Of anything you would rather forget
I want to intuit what you don't share
And sense your mystery
I don't want to rewrite our history

Or reclaim your story as my own
I don't want to write just because I feel so alone
I don't want to write poems about who we were
Never were
Could've been
If I'd just seen the signs
If I'd just been in the right place at the right time
To receive all you were trying to give
I don't want to write poems like that
But this is how I live.